Captivating

Object Lessons

WESLEY T. RUNK

BAKER BOOK HOUSE
GRAND RAPIDS, MICHIGAN

ISBN: 0-8010-7671-4

Third printing, September 1984

Formerly published under the title,
The Devil Is a Mosquito Bite

Printed in the United States of America

TABLE OF CONTENTS

GOD'S THICK SYRUP

Titus 3:4-7, vs. 6: ". . . which he poured out upon us richly through Jesus Christ our Savior . . . "

Object: some very thick syrup that you would use on waffles or pancakes.

Happy New Year, everybody! It's a brand New Year which we all hope will be the best year that there ever has been for you and me and everyone in the whole world. I think that we should begin the New Year with a special prayer for all of God's people. Will you close your eyes and bow your heads with me?

Dear Lord Jesus, we are your children of peace and love. Make this new year a time when all boys and girls shall learn about you and sing songs of praise and joy. Make every day a new and exciting day when we learn to care about people who need us. Amen.

It sure is good to know that God cares for us and loves us so much, isn't it? I mean, it makes you feel good to know that he wants you to be happy and without worry or fear. God is Love. Isn't that great? The Scriptures say it another way. They say that he poured himself out upon us richly. Do you know what it means when we talk about something being rich? [*Let them answer.*] Those are all pretty good answers, but I have something here that will help you to remember the things that the Bible teaches us about God.

How many of you have ever eaten a waffle or a pancake? Oh, boy, do I like pancakes! I like to put butter on each pancake and then take something that I keep in this bottle and pour it over my pancakes thickly. What do you call that? Syrup, that's right, and when I put it on pancakes I just pour it out until it covers the pancakes an inch thick. Boy, that's rich! It looks rich, doesn't it? [*By now you will have filled a cup or a plate with your syrup.*]

That's the way it is with God. He doesn't give a little bit of himself to us, but a whole bunch, more than we deserve. But God wants to make sure that we have enough, and that we understand him. Jesus didn't just tell us about God; he was God. Jesus didn't just get up from being dead and go away. He sent us the Holy Spirit so that we would never feel alone or separated from God. When God does something for us, he does it richly. When he made the world, he made it the most beautiful world with plenty of air, water, and ground. He made plenty of trees and grass and all of the other things that we might ever need. God also did some other things richly, like dying and forgiving our sins. When Jesus died, he did it for all of our sins. Not for just a few people, but for everybody. When God does something, he does it richly, just like pouring maple syrup on pancakes. Now, the next time that you think about God doing something in the world for you and for anybody else, you remember how he does it. He pours it out richly.

SUCH A WASTE!

Romans 12:1-5, vs. 3: For by the grace given to me I bid every one among you not to think of himself more highly than he ought to think, but to think with sober judgment, each according to the measure of faith which God has assigned him.

Object: a drinking glass, a pitcher of water, and a pan to set it into.

Good morning, boys and girls, and how are you this morning? It is certainly a pleasant day in God's House. How I love to come to the church on Sunday morning and know that I am going to greet you in the name of Jesus. It must be fun to get up and think about being with your friends on the Lord's Day. On the other hand, it is good to get up any morning and think about friends. When we think about each other, we don't think so much about ourselves, and that is good. Did you know that St. Paul wrote to the people in Rome and told them not to think too much about themselves and especially not to think too highly about themselves. It's easy to think about yourself. If we don't watch out, the first thing that we know we are saying to ourselves, "I sure am pretty," or "I sure am smarter than anybody else." That is what Paul means about thinking too highly about ourselves.

There is another way, of course, to show you what I mean. Suppose, for instance, that my good friend Glenda Glass came to my house and asked for a glass of water. Now, I know that you may not know my friend Glenda, but she is one of those people who think a lot of themselves. Oh, my, when you start talking to Glenda, the only thing that she really ever seems to think about is herself. Let me tell you what I mean. Glenda came over to my house and she asked for a drink of water. Well, there isn't anything wrong with that, so I went into the kitchen to get her filled up, but she said to me, "Get a big pitcher full of water." I started to pour a little bit into her. "Pour it all in," she said. Glenda thought so much of herself that she believed she could take the whole big pitcher of water into herself. I tried to talk her out of it, but it just wouldn't work. She wanted it all. [*Take the pitcher and pour it all out into the glass.*] Well, as you might have guessed, the pitcher of water was just too much for Glenda. Now that is what I mean about some-body thinking too much of herself. It is such a waste.

God doesn't want us to think too much about our-selves because, if we do, then we not only cause a lot of waste, but there is so little time left over for others. From now on I don't want anybody spending his time thinking about himself when he could be helping others. Just remember Glenda and you know what I mean. She was just another glass, she was never a big pitcher. You are one of God's people, but you are not all of God's people. Don't think too highly of yourself and God will be pleased with you.

TODAY'S TALENT SHOW

Romans 12:6-16a, vs. 6: Having gifts that differ according to the grace given to us, let us use them.

Object: a drawing pad and pencil, a song, a poem, or anything else that you would like to have a child perform.

This morning I am looking for all of the talented people in our congregation, but I am especially looking for talented young people. Just to show you that I am not kidding, I have lined up some of the things that young people can do very well. For instance, I have a poem that I would like someone to read, and a song for someone else to sing, and a pad for someone to draw a picture on. I know that these are things that young people do very well. Now, while you are thinking about what you want to do, I want to tell you why I am suggesting this.

We call these things that we are able to do talents or gifts, and they come from God. Just as we all look different, so we all can do different things. For instance, I know some men who like to preach, but others would rather heal sick people. Some big girls that I know want only to be mothers, while others like to work in an office, or teach school. These are gifts, real gifts from God, and he expects us to use them.

Now, who would like to sing a song? Fine, here is the music and I know that you will do a good job. [*Make sure that it is a familiar song.*] While she is looking at her music, would someone like to read over this poem, and someone else who likes to draw start drawing either a house or a horse or an airplane? That will be fine, and remember that, whatever you do, you are doing it because God has given you the ability to do it.

I understand that this young man is the champion somersaulter in our church. [*Pick out one of the littlest ones for this.*] Would you turn a somersault and remember when you do it that it is a gift from God to be able to turn such a good somersault. And there is one other thing. I understand that this young lady loves to make people happy with her laugh. Would you laugh a little bit so we can see how happy you make other people feel? That was terrific.

Now, let's hear the others. [*Take the others one by one and let them use their gifts.*]

That sure was good. It is wonderful the way that you use your gifts. God is thrilled by the way that you use your talents. I hope you never forget that everybody can do something well because that is the way that God made us. It doesn't make any difference what the gift is if we use it to help each other and praise God. So, read or write or draw or sing or just laugh and make people happy and you will be doing the thing that God wants you to do with the gift he gave you.

DON'T BE A SNOB

Romans 12:16b-21, vs. 16b: Do not be haughty, but associate with the lowly; never be conceited.

Object: a horn.

Are there any conceited people here this morning? Is there anyone here who likes to brag a lot? Would all of the people who think they are better than anyone else please come up and stand beside me so that we can see the people who like to talk about themselves more than anything else? Isn't that strange that there are few here, hardly any at all, who like to brag, or think of themselves as being conceited? We make jokes about conceited people and say that they have fat or big heads. [*Describe this by holding your hands up to your face and moving them out to show this big face.*]

Sometimes we also say that these kind of people have lots of hot air. But, my favorite thought about the haughty, which means being a snob, or the conceited, is to tell them to go blow a horn. [*Show your horn.*] That's right, I just tell them to save their wind and blow their horn instead of telling me how good they are. If they are going to make noise, they might as well play a horn instead of making me listen to them tell me how pretty they are, or how strong they are, or maybe how tough they are. The conceited person feels like he must tell you this because what he has done is so small that he is afraid you will miss it.

Now, St. Paul says that we should never be like that. We don't need horn blowers in the Church of Jesus Christ because we know that everything that needs to be done is done, or has been done by Jesus Christ. That's right, Jesus either does the work for us or gives us the gifts with which it can be done. A good carpenter knows that he receives his talent to work with wood from God. A doctor doesn't brag that he cured a sick man, but instead he knows that God gave him a great talent to heal.

St. Paul says that we should live and work with those who are lowly, and that means to be with people who don't think too much of themselves, but instead think a lot about God and God's people. That's the kind of boys and girls that belong in our church. We want you to be thinking and helping others and not standing around blowing a horn. What we need is more workers and fewer horn blowers.

Now, you understand why God doesn't want you to be conceited or to be a snob. You are just kidding yourself if you think that you are better than someone else. God made us all and he never thought about making some better than others. God says, "Do the job — don't be a snob."

THE EMPTY PILLOW CASE

Romans 13:8-10, vs. 10: Love does no wrong to a neighbor, therefore, love is the fulfilling of the law.

Object: an empty pillowcase and a pillow.

Good morning, boys and girls. Do you ever get a chance to say good morning to one another? Why don't you just say, "Good morning, my friend" right now to one another? That was fine. Sometimes we forget to say nice things to each other, don't we?

This morning I have brought with me a wonderful friend called Patty. Patty is quite a girl. As a matter of fact, Patty has a middle and last name that are kind of funny. Her name is Patty Pillow Case. Patty is a nice friend, but there is something wrong with her. I don't know what it is, but it seems that Patty is missing something. I have checked her all over and she seems to be all right, but I have a funny feeling. She is sewed in all of the right places, and she has a front and a back, and she is open at one end, just like a good pillowcase should be, but Patty reminds me of a promise that has not been kept. There is something missing. Is there anyone here who can figure what is missing? What should a good, honest, respectable pillowcase have that Patty Pillow Case doesn't. [*Wait for someone to say a pillow.*] Of course, a pillow. No wonder Patty seemed like a promise that had not been kept. How many of you like to sleep on pillowcases without pillows? None of you. How many would like to sleep on Patty Pillow Case if there were a pillow inside her? You would? All of you? Well, I don't blame you.

Did you know that the law is like a pillowcase and that love is like a pillow? That's right. A pillowcase is like a promise that someday it will be good to sleep on, but a pillow is like keeping that promise. You can sleep on a pillow, but a pillowcase is just a hope. Before Jesus came we had the law, and the law promised certain things, but when Jesus came, the promise was filled. That is the way love works. The law tells you to be good. Love fills your heart and you are good. The law tells you to be kind. Love fills you so that you want to be kind. The love of God that Jesus brings and gives us makes us full just like our pillows fill our pillowcases and make them wonderful places to sleep.

When I put my pillow into Patty Pillow Case, she is filled and then I know that she is complete. Now, there is nothing missing. You were meant to be filled with love, the real love of God, and when you have love you are full. With love inside you, like a pillow in a pillowcase, you have joy, hope, kindness, strength, gentleness, understanding, and many other things that love brings. So ask Jesus for his love and you will be made as full as Patty. With love inside you, there will be nothing missing.

THE MOST IMPORTANT PRIZE

1 Corinthians 9:24-10:5, vs. 24: Do you not know that in a race all the runners compete, but only one receives the prize? So run that you may obtain it.

Object: trophies of any kind.

Good morning, boys and girls. This is the first Sunday in the shortest month of the year. How many of you know what month this is that we are now living in? And who can tell me how many days there are in this month? [*Let them answer the questions.*] That's right, there are [twenty-eight] days and the name of the month is February. This month can get over in a hurry. If there was ever a race between months to see which one could finish first, it would be no contest. That's right. February would finish first every time.

Speaking of races, is there anyone here this morning who is fast? I mean, is there anyone here who has been in a race and has won? Terrific! What do you get when you finish a race and everyone is behind you? [*Again let them answer.*] A prize. What kind of a prize do you receive? [*Ribbons, candy, etc.*] Did you know that in the big races where men from different schools or countries run and set the world records, they receive something like this? [*Hold up the trophy.*] That's right, the fastest men in the world win trophies and they are proud of them. At least they are proud of them for a while. Pretty soon the winner wins another race and then another race and another and another, and the first trophy that he got may seem a little old or small or unimportant. It just seems to fade away. Prizes and trophies are nice, but they don't seem to last a long time.

Now, St. Paul must have gone to a lot of races and other athletic events, because he liked to talk about them in his letters. He thinks that a Christian should train himself in faith as an athlete trains his body. We should exercise our faith and try different and new ways to test it. We should also remember St. Paul says that there is a prize for every Christian at the end of his life. You have to wait a long time for it and there is only one trophy or prize, and not a bunch of them; but it is worth training for it. St. Paul says that the Christian will receive a prize that will be more **important** than all of the trophies that the fastest runner in the world has ever won. How many of you know what the prize is for the Christian with great faith? [*See what kind of answers you get.*] Life, eternal life is the prize. It is a gift from God for all the people who use the faith that God gives them in this life. St. Paul says that such a gift is far more important than any other prize. So, you can see why Christians want to be faithful to God here on earth. They want the free gift of eternal life so that they can live forever in peace with God.

A TERRIFIC SINGER

2 Corinthians 11:19-12:9, vs. 12:6: Though if I wish to boast, I shall not be a fool, for I shall be speaking the truth. But I refrain from it, so that no one may think more of me than he sees in me or hears from me.

Object: a tape recorder.

Today we want to talk about something that you hear about once in a while — it is called boasting. How many of you know something about boasting? Do you know what it means to boast? [*Let them answer.*] That's right, it means to brag. I guess we all brag once in a while, but when we do, it is not very attractive and it never sounds very good. We do all kinds of bragging and some of it is even true. It better be true or otherwise you are in real trouble. That's what St. Paul said when he wrote to the people in Corinth. If you boast or brag, you had better be able to back it up with the truth. When you don't, you are in real trouble.

For instance, I like to brag once in a while about my lovely voice. Oh, I have a great voice. When people hear me sing they say, "Have you ever heard such a voice." Other people say, "What a voice!" Of course, I sing a lot. I sing very high notes and I sing very low notes. Then there are the songs that I sing. Why, I sing some of the most beautiful songs that you have ever heard. I sing all of the old songs and all of the new songs. I sing fast songs and slow songs. I also sing in some very famous places and in some not so famous places. But do you know where I sing best? I sing best when I sing in the shower or bathtub. Then I am just terrific! I sing high and low and fast and slow. I am a terrific singer. I suppose that you want to hear me sing now. Well, I have such a delicate voice that I thought I would just bring along my tape recorder so that you could hear me sing that way. [*Play the tape recorder with some beautiful recording of a man singing.*] How did you like that? I suppose that you still want me to sing, don't you? Now, you have to remember that this is early in the morning and I don't sound just like I did on the tape. [*Sing a few bars of "Row, Row, Row Your Boat"*] Oh, my, I don't sound very good. That means that I shouldn't have boasted so much. That's the trouble with bragging. Now, none of you will think that I am a very good singer.

That's why St. Paul says that we should not brag at all. We should let other people tell about us and what they see and hear of us doing. People like St. Paul never have to brag because they let other people watch what they do. They would never tell you how good they can sing. They would just sing and let you decide if you like it or thought it was good. So, we want you to remember that boasting or bragging is not a good thing. Just do your best and let people know you from the good things others say about you.

A CLANGING CYMBAL

1 Corinthians 13:1-13, vs. 1: If I speak in the tongues of men and of angels, but have not love, I am a noisy gong or a clanging cymbal.

Object: a cymbal (borrowed from an orchestra at school).

BANG! BANG! BANG [*Begin with the clanging of the cymbals.*] WOW! How did you like that for the beginning of a children's sermon? How would you like to talk to someone who made a noise like this every time he talked? BANG, BANG, BANG! It is kind of fun to do it once or even twice, but can you imagine doing it every few minutes? Instead of saying, "Good morning, and how are you?" you would only hear six bangs from these cymbals. That is kind of frightening, but that is what St. Paul says some people sound like when they talk. Now you might say, "What kind of person talks like that? I have never heard anyone make noises like a cymbal." Well, people who talk like that are people who speak without love. They have no love and so they simply rattle and bang around causing other people problems and heartaches.

Love is what makes the Christian a real person, a follower of God. Without love, he is just like everyone else, but with love he becomes something very special. For instance, when he talks he speaks to you about the things that you want to talk about and not just about what he did or wants to do. He wants to know how you really feel and what has happened that makes you feel so good. He never tries to hurt you with gossip or dirty talk. He speaks to you about the wonderful things that God has done and how much God loves you. When the Christian speaks, it is never like a clanging cymbal, but like beautiful music or like a flowing poem.

Love is God's special gift to people. It is not "gooey" or "mushy," for it takes real courage sometimes to be able to love. Just think how you might act toward a person who has called you names, and has said some very insulting things about you. If you did not have the love which God gave you to use, you would shout back and sound like this clanging cymbal and then you would have many other hurt people. No, because you are a Christian, you will not sound like this (BANG!!) clanging cymbal, but instead you will speak like an angel and you will bring love and happiness where there was hate before. Cymbals are for orchestras and not for people, God's people.

DO NOT ENTER

2 Corinthians 6:1-10, vs. 3: We put no obstacle in any one's way, so that no fault may be found with our ministry.

Object: a big piece of chain and a sign with the words "Do Not Enter."

Good morning, boys and girls. Have you ever ridden in a car with your mother or father and seen this sign? [*Hold up the "Do Not Enter" sign.*] You are just about to turn into this street when you have to put on your brakes and stop. The place you want to go is right up that block, but they won't let you go past the sign because the street is torn up, or it is one way, the other way. That sign is an obstacle. It keeps us from going where we want to go.

I need a couple of volunteers for another obstacle that I brought with me. [*Take out the chain. Have them take the ends and stretch it out across the chancel.*] Now, here is an obstacle. What do you call this? That's right, a chain, and when they stretch big chains like this, it means that you can go no farther. It means you must stop right here. Sometimes these obstacles are for your safety, and then they are good; but sometimes there are other obstacles that are bad and they only hurt. Did you know that you can be an obstacle? That's right. I know some people who keep other people from being Christians. St. Paul says that we must be very careful and never get in the way of other people who want to be Christians. For instance, I know some boys and girls who talk meanly to each other and still call themselves Christians. When other boys and girls see them talk that way they say, "I don't want to be like them; they talk meanly to each other. If that is a Christian, I don't want to be one." When you talk meanly, it is just like holding up a sign that says "Do Not Enter" or "We Don't Want You to Be Christians." If you lie or cheat or hurt other people or show that you do not love God, it is just like stretching a chain which says, "This is an obstacle that you cannot pass through."

So, remember, you can be an obstacle that can hurt and keep people from knowing God. Or you can be a path, a big wide street or a six-lane highway that lets people come to know God better and love him more than they ever did before. When you show people how much fun it is to love and be happy and joyful, and you tell them that it is because you believe in Jesus, then they will want to be Christians, too. So, please, don't be an obstacle, but, instead, be a six-lane highway.

LITTLE REPEATERS

1 Thessalonians 4:1-7, vs. 1: Finally, brethren, we beseech and exhort you in the Lord Jesus that as you learned from us, how you ought to live and to please God, just as you are doing, you do so more and more.

Object: yo-yo, paddle with ball attached, or multiplication tables — anything that you only learn with great repetition.

Good morning, my little repeaters. How many of you know what it means to repeat? [*Wait for an answer.*] It means to do something again, and there are some things that we like to do again and again, and some things that we do not like to do over. For instance, I think that most of you like to be repeaters when it comes to eating hamburgers and french fries. On the other hand, most of you do not like to eat spinach or to take the time to wash your face and hands more than once a day. But, we are all repeaters and did you know why? Because, when we do something over and over again, we learn to do it better each time.

I brought along some of my friends today whom I thought most of you would like to meet. First of all, I have my pal Yancy Yo-Yo. Now, Yancy is a good friend, but I occasionally have some problems with him. I am sure that you all know what Yancy is supposed to do, don't you? [*Let them answer.*] Right, that is what he is supposed to do, but watch. [*Try a couple of times to show that you can't make it go very well.*] Of course, that isn't the only friend who works fairly slowly. Here is Peter Paddle. Peter used to swat the ball so well that he would wear out the rubber band and we would have to replace it. Not now! Why, Peter hardly even touches the ball when I use him. Oh, I know what you are saying. You are thinking to yourself, "It isn't Peter and Yancy who are wrong, but the Pastor who is goofing it up." You know what? You're right. I am goofing it up because I haven't been practicing with Peter and Yancy. You have to do it every day and not just once in a while if you want to keep these two friends, Yancy and Peter, happy.

I suppose that you know why I am telling you this story. St. Peter wrote to some Christians in Thessalonica and told them that they were doing a fine job with the Christian teachings that he had given them, but they were not to stop at that point. No, he said, you must do what is right over and over again and that must be every day. If you stop doing what is right, you will forget, and the next thing you know, it will be the wrong thing that you are doing. Just like with Yancy and Peter. You must work with them every day. So, Paul says, do something good for someone every day. Pray often, love your enemy, give food to the hungry, and so forth. That is the way we learn to be Christians: by practicing every day. Just think how good I will be with Peter and Yancy if I practice every day this week. You can be a real Christian, if you practice your faith as much as I am going to practice with my friends.

JUST BE LIKE JESUS

Ephesians 5:1-9, vs. 6: Let no one deceive you with empty words, for it is because of these things that the wrath of God comes upon the sons of disobedience.

Object: a nearly empty tube (such as toothpaste), or a picture frame with a picture of a monkey, or a crayon box without crayons.

Who likes to be tricked? Sometimes it's fun, but most of the time we don't like to be tricked. We especially don't like to be tricked if we know that other people are trying to trick us. If I asked someone here to draw me a beautiful picture of a horse and there wasn't a horse to draw, you would think I was tricking you, wouldn't you? [*Select someone.*] OK, I don't care what you draw, just so that it is pretty. [*Hand her the crayon box without any crayons. After she opens it . . .*] See what I mean! Sometimes people try to trick us. There are other times when something happens that no one meant to have happen. For instance, it seems like every time I go to brush my teeth, the person in my family who was there before me used the last bit of toothpaste and left an empty tube. [*Squeeze the tube or use an empty salt shaker or sugar bowl.*] There are other things that happen to me that are mean, like the boy who had his picture taken [*Select a boy*] and gave it to me for a present. Wasn't that awful of Tommy to give me his picture as a present. Why did he think that I wanted his picture? [*Turn it around and show them the picture of the monkey.*] Wasn't that a trick, a mean trick? See, if I keep talking and doing things like this, you won't like me and you will never believe me again.

Am I mean? Not really. I only did this to show you what God wants us to learn from his holy Word this morning. God says that we should not try to trick people or let people trick us with empty words or promises. St.

Paul says that God really gets angry when some people try to make other people think that God is not love or that he does not forgive or that he makes false promises. That is not the way that God works or teaches us to work. He says to be honest and to imitate him, and not to deceive or lead people away from him. Now, sometimes we do wrong and we are sorry and we ask his forgiveness and God forgives us. But there are other times when we try to get other people to do wrong things like we are doing, and we are not sorry; but God says that we are going to be sorry if we don't change. So, you remember what St. Paul said and try to be more like God, doing the things that he wants us to do. And, remember to be careful of people who might trick you into being bad. Just be like Jesus: imitate him.

IS FREE JUST LOOSE?

Galatians 4:21-5:1a, vs. 5:1a: For freedom Christ has set us free.

Object: a wristwatch or a pocket watch on a chain.

Good morning, boys and girls, and how are you today? Did you get up this morning filled with God's love and joy? Are you very glad to be alive? Is that the way that you got up this morning? Very good! When you got up this morning, did you also thank God for being free? [*Wait for some answers.*] What does it mean to be free?

Is free being loose? Suppose I grab [*Take one of the boys who wouldn't be frightened*] Jim and just hold him so that he cannot get away, or hold Susan's hands so tightly that she cannot move them and then let them go, are they now free? Is that what we mean by being free? To be free is more than being loose.

Let me show you a little experiment. Here is my good old faithful friend, Willie Watch. Now, Willie may not feel free because I keep him tied to my wrist. That's right, Willie goes no farther than around my wrist and I keep him right there most of the time. Now, Willie is a good watch and he keeps excellent time, but he keeps telling me that he is a slave and that I never let him be free. He doesn't mind his job. He does it well and likes to say tick-tock, tick-tock. Suppose I let Willie go. I will just take him off from my wrist and let whatever happens to him happen. [*Let Willie fall to the floor.*] I will not wind him, polish him, or do anything at all. Willie will be free, at least loose. Do you think that Willie will like it? Of course not.

When the Bible says that Jesus makes us free, it doesn't mean that he cuts us loose. It means instead that he allows us to be at our best. Some people think that Jesus makes us loose, but that isn't real freedom. No, real freedom is when we can do the things that are best.

My friend Willie was really free when he was right here on my wrist, working, making his tick-tock noise and telling the right time for everybody. That is what Jesus does when he makes everything right between you and God. He makes you free. You don't have to worry about your sins anymore. You can work and play without being afraid, because you are one of God's children. You are free, really free, because you belong to God. That's the same way it is with Willie. He doesn't have to worry any more, because he is free when he belongs to me.

JESUS BRINGS US TOGETHER

Hebrews 9:11-15, vs. 15: Therefore, he is the mediator of a new covenant, so that those who are called may receive the promised eternal inheritance, since a death has occurred which redeems them from the transgressions under the first covenant.

Object: a stapler and two pieces of paper.

Good morning, boys and girls. Today is a good day for us to be together. I like things to be together. Do you know what I mean? For instance, I like to sit down at a table where the knife and the fork and the spoon are beside the plate and not on the cupboard or on a chair. They belong with the plate. I feel the same way about a coat and hat. I like to see the coat and the hat where they belong on a person and not wrapped around the feet or hanging on a hook.

Did you know that God is like that also? He likes things to be where they belong and not somewhere else. For instance, God had a plan for all of his people in this world and it was that they would live here on earth with him and be very happy. But the people didn't seem to like God's plan and they decided that they would like to try out their own plan and be like God. They thought that they knew as much and could do as much as God could do, so they told God that they were going to do it their own way. Well, you can guess what happened. Things really got in a mess and pretty soon the people on earth were very sorry that they had decided to try to live without God. Lucky for the people, God did not give up on them, for when they asked for help he was right there waiting. Now God tried a lot of things to help the people come back and live right with him, but they were so used to fighting with each other doing things wrong that it didn't seem to make any difference. He gave them the Ten Commandments and they tried for a while, but it just didn't seem to work. God sent prophets and named special men kings but they still seemed to only want to do things their own way. Finally, God had a wonderful plan that he knew would work. I want to show you that plan with my friend Stanley Stapler. Stanley had two pieces of paper that he wanted to bring together, so he just sent a staple out that fixed these two pieces of paper in such a way that they could not come loose. The staple holds them together, and the two pieces of paper get along just fine.

Well, that is the way that God did it. He sent his son Jesus into the world just as Stanley sent the staple. And sure enough, God brought us together. The Bible calls Jesus the mediator. It is Jesus who brings us together and makes us part of God's world again. Now, we don't have to worry because God's plan works so well that we can go to God anytime and pray in the name of Jesus. Just like the staple brings two pieces of paper together, so Jesus brings God and boys and girls together. So, the next time you see a staple, you will remember that it is a mediator just as Jesus is your mediator. A staple can only bring paper together, but Jesus can bring you and God together.

JESUS GAVE HIMSELF

Philippians 2:5-11, vss. 6 and 7: . . . who, though he was in the form of God, did not count equality with God a thing to be grasped, but emptied himself, taking the form of a servant being born in the likeness of men.

Object: two candles, one burned and the other brand new (they should be the same kind of candles to begin with).

Good morning, boys and girls, and how are you on this great Christian day called Palm Sunday? How many of you remember the story of Palm Sunday? What kind of picture comes to your mind when you think of Palm Sunday? [*Let them answer.*] What a wonderful picture Jesus must have been riding down the streets of Jerusalem with the people shouting and singing loud Hosannas and covering the streets with palm branches and coats. Jesus is someone you can never forget once you have heard about him.

People used to wonder how anyone could be so perfect and still look like other people and live with other people. Sometimes we still wonder about that and ask ourselves how Jesus could be God and suffer and die like a man. I mean, if he were God, he should not be like a man, and if he is a man then we shouldn't expect him to be a God. But we do, and I'll show you what I mean.

Here is a candle, a beautiful white candle that has been sitting on my piano at home for a long time. It looks so good that it makes my whole room look warm and beautiful. This is the way I think a candle should look and whenever someone mentions a candle, I think of this beautiful white candle that sits on my piano. Now I have another candle, and at one time this other candle was as big and beautiful as my piano candle. But we needed light and we needed the light badly one night when we had an awful storm and there was a power failure and the lights went out. So I took the candle down from the piano and struck a match and lit the candle. It burned and burned for as long as it was needed. You might say that the candle gave itself for us. The candle was not concerned if it stayed tall and beautiful, but wanted best to burn so that we might have light and plenty of it.

Well, that is the way that it is with Jesus. As God, he is as big as he wants to be and as beautiful, but when we were in so much trouble because of our sin, he came and gave himself up, even when it cost him his life on the cross. Jesus is like the candle that gave its light, even though in being burned it grew smaller instead of staying big and beautiful. God was in Jesus even though he looked like a person and eventually even died a cruel death. God was in him and he gave himself so that we might have life and have it abundantly.

WHAT GOD KEEPS IN HEAVEN FOR YOU

1 Peter 1:3-9, vss. 3b and 4: By his great mercy we have been born anew to a living hope through the resurrection of Jesus Christ from the dead, and to an inheritance **which** *is imperishable, undefiled, and unfading, kept in heaven for you.*

Object: a savings bond or an insurance policy for college.

Happy Easter, everybody! Isn't this the most wonderful day in the whole year? You feel so free and easy. There is nothing in the world to worry about, since we know that Jesus has won over everything, including the devil himself. It wasn't always like this, I can tell you that. There was a time when people lived in absolute fear of dying. But not anymore! The grave used to be such a horrible thought that people wouldn't even talk about it to each other. Today, we know that it is all different, and I think that I can show you what I mean.

[*Hold up the savings bond.*] Have you ever seen one of these, boys and girls? [*Ask them if anyone has ever heard about or seen a savings bond.*] You haven't? I know that you have learned about them, for this is a savings bond. A lot of your parents have bought these and are keeping them for a very special time in your life. Parents buy savings bonds from our government and put them in the bank for ten years, or even longer, and when it is time for you to go to college or do something special when you grow up, they have the money ready for you. They keep it in the bank and never spend it until the right time comes for you to need it.

The reason that I tell you this is that this is the reason Jesus died for you and for all people so many years ago. You remember how I told you that people used to be afraid of dying because it seemed to be the end of nowhere else to go? And do you remember that Jesus died on the cross for our sins? You do? Well, you must also know, then, that Jesus was raised from the dead by his heavenly Father and made alive again. And that is not all! The Father in Heaven promised Jesus that, because Jesus lives again, we who believe in Jesus will also live in a special place in heaven. Jesus is keeping that place for us for a special time, just as your folks keep a savings bond for you for a very special time. The only thing is that, as special as your parent's gift is for you, the gift of eternal life given by Jesus is the most precious gift of all. Isn't that great? None of us has to worry ever again about dying because Jesus has a special place for all of us. Hallelujah!

BALLOONS!

1 John 5:4-12, vs. 12: He who has the Son has life; he who has not the Son of God has not life.

Object: balloons, enough for each child and something to pump them up (or have them pre-filled).

Have you ever seen a light bulb that was burned out, or tried to use a pencil that didn't have any lead or a ballpoint pen without ink? If you have ever seen or tried to use any one of these items, you know how disappointing it really is. You don't know that the light bulb is burned out until you try to use it, and the same thing is true with the others. How many times I have tried to make an old ballpoint pen work, and it just won't. All of these things have good bodies, but there is no life left in them.

Let me show you something else that works that way. What is this? [*Hold up the balloon.*] That's right, a balloon. Or is it a balloon? What are balloons supposed to be able to do? [*Wait for some answers.*] That's right, they should be able to float around in the air and, if taken outside and let go where the wind can get them, they will fly away high in the sky. I love a balloon when you can do those kinds of things with them. But, look at this so-called balloon. If I let it go, it will just drop to the floor like a piece of dead weight. It needs something to make it a real balloon. Does anyone here know what it is? That's right, air, my air or your air blown into it will make it a real balloon. Let's try it. [*Blow up a balloon.*] See what I mean. Now it is a real balloon.

It is the same way with people. Some people look like people and we call them people because we think that they are alive. But, the Bible tells us that they are not alive unless they have the Son of God, meaning Jesus, within them. Without Jesus they are like a pen without ink or a light bulb without light. But really those people

are more like a balloon, because once the pen is without
ink you just throw it away and the light bulb you just
break; but with a balloon you can always put more air
into it. People sometimes forget what Jesus wants of
them, and they leave him out of their lives; but, even
though that is bad it is not the end of the line like a
broken light bulb. We need Jesus to be alive just like the
balloon needs air, the pen needs ink, and the pencil needs
lead. But Jesus says to us that it is never too late or the
wrong time for him to make you alive. Even if you have
forgotten him for awhile you can have him back if you
just invite him, and he will be to you like fresh air is to a
balloon.

PATTERNED AFTER JESUS

1 Peter 2:21b-25, vs. 21: For to this you have been called, because Christ also suffered for you, leaving you an example, that you should follow in his steps.

Object: an office punch (hole punch) and different shapes and colors of paper.

How many times have you wished that you could be like Jesus? Wouldn't it be wonderful to be able to live like Jesus lived and do good things for people, like healing the ones who are sick, and making the sad very happy, and giving right answers to whatever questions are asked? Jesus was a wonderful person to know and all the disciples and people who knew him thought so.

[*Take out the first piece of paper and the punch.*] You know that, when Jesus lived here on earth, he had a special way of living and he asked all of the people who trusted him to be a lot like him. [*Punch a hole for each thing that you mention that he did.*] I mean, Jesus prayed and he wanted us to pray; Jesus did kind things for people and he wanted us to do kind things for people; Jesus never returned a hurt for a hurt; Jesus kept his promises and wanted us to keep our promises. Now those are just a few of the things that Jesus did, but look what happens when we are the same way. [*Take another piece of paper and begin to punch holes in that sheet using the Jesus paper as a pattern.*] If we use Jesus as an example and his life as a pattern, then we also will pray and do kind things for people and never try to hurt others, and we will keep our promises. Now, look at what happens when we follow Jesus. Even though we may be a different shape and have a different color, we can be a lot like him. When we follow Jesus like this, we are called Christians because we show others that our example for living is Jesus.

Let me show you one other thing about what happens when we make Jesus our example and try to live as he wants us to live. If I take some string and put it through the holes of both the Jesus paper and the other paper, we can see that they match, that they belong together. That's what we all want and what Jesus wants for us, to belong to one another. If we live like he lived and try to be as much like him as we can, we will not only make God happy and others happy, but we will be happier ourselves.

TURN OFF THE WORLD — WITH LOVE!

1 Peter 2:11-20, vs. 15: For this is God's will: he wants you to silence the ignorant talk of foolish men by the good things you do.

Object: a teakettle.

Good morning, boys and girls. One of my favorite times of the week is Sunday when I can be together with you early in the morning. Sometimes I think of a story to tell you very early in the week and then I have to wait for days to tell you about it. The good thing about today is that I don't have to wait any longer to tell you about a friend whom I brought along with me to help me tell you something that St. Peter said a long time ago.

See who I brought with me? This is an old friend of mine, and a noisy one, too. [*Hold up the teakettle.*] Her name is Tillie Teakettle and she is quite a girl. Old Tillie has done a lot of work in her time and once in a while you might say she has blown her stack. By the way, Tillie asked me if I would check to see if any of her relatives lived in your houses. If you have a teakettle at your house, it might be one of her aunts or uncles or even a cousin. If you have one, will you please raise your hand? Wonderful! Tillie is pleased about that.

I told you that Tilly has blown her stack on more than one occasion and when she does, everyone knows it. It kind of bothers me, because she screams so loudly that she is finished doing her job. How many of you know what kind of whistle Tillie makes when she gets hot? [*Here you can demonstrate with a shrill whistle or let the whole group do so together.*] That's kind of what she sounds like and she just keeps on doing it until you turn her off.

The reason that I am telling you this story is that Peter says the world is a lot like Tillie, because of the way it treats Christians. Sometimes, Peter says, you have to turn the world off just like you turn off Tillie. When people tell you that they don't pray, or worship, or attend Sunday School, or do any of the other things that we like to do to show the Lord Jesus how much we love him, we have to turn them off. Now, we can't do that to the world like we can turn off Tillie, so Peter tells us another way. He says that, as Christians, we must turn them off with love. We don't hit back when they hit us. No, we ask how we can help them. When they eat all of their candy and don't give us any, we don't keep all our candy to ourselves. No, we share it with them. We Christians always do good for those who try to hurt us and that is the way that we turn them off or change them.

The next time that you see Tillie Teakettle, you remember what St. Peter taught us to do. Turn the world off with kindness and love and everyone will be better because of it.

GOD NEVER CHANGES

*James 1:17-21, vs. 17: Every good endowment and every
perfect gift is from above, coming down from the Father
of lights with whom there is no variation or shadow due
to change.*

*Object: a strong light, a white sheet, finger shadows
made from different angles.*

Good morning, boys and girls. We have talked a lot
about change lately, and we have spoken about how good
it is for us. Sometimes we think that changing is painful,
but we still have to do it because it is better for us in the
long run. Every day brings change, and we often can't do
anything about it. For instance, you can't stop your hair
from getting longer when it grows, or your feet from
changing sizes. They just change. Everything changes
except one thing and I am sure that you can guess what
doesn't change. [*Let them guess.*] That's right, God
doesn't change.

Let me show you what I am talking about. Here is an
ordinary flashlight which I am sure that most of you have
in your homes, and a piece of very white paper. Now I am
going to shine this light on my hand which is close to the
paper and make a what? [*Let them guess.*] That's right, a
shadow. If I were very clever I could make shadows that
looked like dogs or cats or rabbits, but for right now I am
just going to make a shadow. Now I need a volunteer.
[*Select someone to help you who would not ordinarily
volunteer.*] I want my volunteer to hold the flashlight at
different places but still shine it on my hand. Do you see
what happens to the shadow? It gets longer and shorter
and sometimes if you are not careful where you are
shining it you can't see it at all. The shadow is always
changing because the light is always changing.

Now, God made the light and the paper and even the
hand and, while all of these things change, the One who

made them does not change at all. God doesn't change. You change, the light changes, and the shadow changes, but God doesn't change.

Is it good for God not to change? It surely is, because you know now and you always will know that God is love and that God is always forgiving, and that God will never change into anything else but the way that he is today. You and I may change so that we understand him better, but God will not change.

Now, the next time you see a shadow on the sidewalk or in your yard, you can say that it reminds you about the way that God is and always has been. You will say, "The light changes, the shadow changes, but God never changes. He loves me today, tomorrow, and forever."

LISTENING IS NOT ENOUGH

James 1:22-27, vs. 22: But be doers of the word, and not hearers only, deceiving yourselves.

Object: an exercise record, or you can simply make up your own set of exercises that you can give at the proper time. To make this work best, you must divide the group in two with some just listening and the others doing the exercises.

Today was the right day for fat people to come to church. That's right, I have a lesson today for all who feel that they have an extra pound or so that they would like to lose in a hurry. Is there anyone here who thinks he is too fat and needs a little help in getting rid of it? [*Take all the volunteers that you can get; the skinnier the better.*] That is terrific. I am going to see that you all lose an ounce or two before you leave. Before losing weight, I am going to let this group of very fat people do some exercising that is really a lot of fun. The other group of people is going to sit and listen to every word, but they must just sit there and do nothing. Use your ears, but don't even lift a finger. Only this group of fat people get to do the exercises.

[*Play the exercise record here if you have one, but first instruct them to listen carefully and do whatever they are instructed to do. If you have your own exercises then the instructions are also very important. Do it for a few minutes so that they know that they have done some exercising.*] Boy, you were great and I know that you have lost at least four ounces.

Now, let's look at the other group and see what has happened to them. Well, I know that they haven't exercised and built up their muscles so they are not any stronger than they were before they came this morning. However, they did watch pretty closely and it will be interesting to see if they could lose any weight just

watching. Is there anyone in this group who thinks they
lost weight while they were watching the other group
doing some exercises? I don't think so. You see we learn
a very valuable lesson when we understand that just
listening is not enough. We have to do what we are
taught as well.

St. James teaches us that we must do what we hear
or otherwise our Christian teaching is lost. If we just
hear that we must be kind and love one another, but we
don't do anything about it, then we are not Christians at
all. Christians are doers like the group that not only heard
the exercises, but did them. Christians are not like the
group that just listened and did nothing. We must
practice our Christianity by doing things that God wants
us to do. You can't lose weight or build muscles just
sitting around and you can't be a Christian if you don't
use the things that God gives you to help others.
Remember, do what you hear God tell you to do and you
will be called Christian.

COUGH DROPS, LIKE LOVE?

1 Peter 4:7b-11, vs. 8: Above all hold unfailing your love for one another, since love covers a multitude of sins.

Object: cough drops, some plain menthol and a lot of different flavored ones.

Good morning, boys and girls. I hope that you feel good this morning. I just love to come to church on Sunday morning when I feel good. Every once in a while I get here and find out that my throat is a little scratchy, or I have a little cough, and then I feel bad. Of course, when that happens I just take a cough drop and suck on it and pretty soon the bad feeling passes away. How many of you take a cough drop when your throat is a little scratchy or you have a cough? Lots of you do.

Has anyone ever told you that cough drops are a lot like love? They haven't? Well, let me show you how they work and then maybe you will understand how cough drops and love are a lot alike. [*Pass out cough drops to the children, but tell them not to put them into their mouths until you tell them to.*] Now, we are all going to have to pretend that we have very scratchy throats, the kind that make you cough and clear your throats a lot. Think of how awful that throat must feel. Are you getting the idea? Pretty sore, isn't it? I tell you I can hardly talk, my throat is getting so scratchy. Now I think to myself when I have such a sore throat with such a bad cough [*Can you all cough a little bit? That's fine.*] that I had better find something for my throat. How many of you are starting to feel the same way that I do? Don't you wish that you had something for your throat, too? You do? Well, it just so happens that I gave you a very special cough drop, and I want you to put it into your mouth right now and begin to suck on it and see if that doesn't help. That's right, see how it begins to make that old sore throat feel better. You see, the cough drop has some very soothing medicine in it that just covers over the spots that hurt in your throat. Now, when you swallow or cough a little bit, your throat won't hurt a bit.

Now, how are cough drops and love alike? Well, St. Peter tells us that love covers a multitude of sins. The cough drop covers the sore places in our throats just like love covers sins. You see, St. Peter says that God knows that we are not perfect, and that sometimes we do things that he doesn't approve of, but if we try always to love everybody and love what we are doing, and love even the things that other people find hard to love, then some of the things that we have done wrong are a little easier for God to understand. That's what St. Peter means when he says that love covers a multitude of sins.

So you see how cough drops and love are a lot alike? Now, the next time that you take a cough drop you can think to yourself, "This is a lot like love, for when I love others I make them feel good just like the cough drop makes me feel good." And you know what? You're right!

Pastor: If you plan to use Acts 2:1-11 next week, be sure to ask children to bring a gift next Sunday.

1,946 CANDLES ON THE BIRTHDAY CAKE!

Acts 2:1-11, vs. 1: When the day of Pentecost had come, they were all together in one place.

Object: candles for each child and anything else that will help to make this a birthday party.

Good morning, boys and girls, and welcome to the birthday party of a 1,946* year old. How about that? When was the last time that you were invited or even heard of attending a birthday party for someone who was 1,946 years old? Never? Well, today you are all invited to this party, because we are going to have one right now. Do you remember that I told you last week to bring a special gift for the church with you this Sunday morning and that I would be most pleased if you brought something that you made? Well, the gift that you brought is for our guest of honor, the one who is 1,946 years old. Does anyone want to guess who the guest of honor is? [*Let them guess who is 1,946 years old today.*] The church, the Christian church is 1,946 years old today. That's who we are going to have a party for this morning.

The church as we know it began in Jerusalem 1,946 years ago on a day called Pentecost. Today is Pentecost and it was on a day like this that people from all over the world gathered together in Jerusalem and heard for the first time the good news about Jesus Christ. Now a lot of them could hardly believe their ears when they heard the things that the Apostles told them, but before the day was over there were at least 3,000 people who believed and were called followers of Jesus.

When the day was over, the church was born and it began a new life that we still have today. Just think, 1,946 years later the church is still living and growing and in some ways it is still like a tiny child.

*1,946 is applicable in 1979. To get the figure in succeeding years, subtract 33 from the year.

I brought with me some candles that I want to give to you. We are not going to light them here in church, but you can light them when you get home and your parents are there to help you. This birthday candle is a reminder that today you spent your day with a church that not only cares about you and loves you, but promises you to be a part of your life forever. The church, Christ's church, is here to teach you, serve you, and provide for you all the things that you think you will need forever.

NO SPECIAL DEALS WITH GOD

Romans 11:33-36, vs. 35: . . . or who has given a gift to him that he might be repaid?

Object: things that might be used as gifts for the family: tie, perfume, necklace, and ball glove.

Good morning, boys and girls, and how are you today? It sure is good to see so many happy faces on such a bright and wonderful day. The last time I saw so many happy faces was the other day when I went to a birthday party. I don't think that I will ever forget how happy the boy was with all his presents. How many of you get presents on your birthday? A lot of you receive gifts. The boys and girls who attended the party got things, too, such as prizes for winning games, and ice cream and cake, and special birthday hats. They got what they wanted, and the boy who had the birthday party got what he wanted, and everyone was happy.

I wish that everyone could be as happy as those boys and girls were. Maybe if I gave everyone a present the whole world would be happy. I could give my father this nice tie and my mother this perfume and my sister a necklace and my brother this ball glove. They sure would be happy. Don't you think that this would make them happy? [*Let them answer.*] You know, I should give gifts to everyone who has made me happy. I think that I will even give God a gift, because he has made me so happy. Don't you think that would be a great idea? Why, if I gave God a gift, just think what he might give me. That is the way you do it, isn't it? If I give God a gift, then he will have to give me a gift in return, won't he? Maybe I could give him Dad's tie or the ball glove. I don't think that God would look very good with a necklace or use perfume. What can I give God? Is there anything that God wants that I can give him? He has given me so much, and I can't think of a thing to give him. Just think of some of the things that God has given me. [*Let them name a few.*] He has done a lot, but what can I give him? He has everything. If I wanted something really good from God, I would have to give him something that would really be special and very expensive. Can you think of something that would really be expensive that I could give to God? [*Lead them to saying gold and silver or diamonds or big buildings.*] Do you think that God would really give me something big in return, if I gave him some gold or diamonds? You don't? Is it because God already owns all the diamonds and gold, and he just lets us use them? That's right. God owns everything, and there is nothing that we can give him that will make him want to pay us back. He doesn't give special favors. God loves us all and gives us everything that we need. The things of this world still belong to him and he lets us use them.

There isn't any gift that we can give that will make us any more special than what we already are to him. God loves us and gives us all things freely. Remember, no special deals with God. He doesn't make them, but he will give you everything that you need for nothing and love you more than you can even imagine.

GOD IS LOVE

*1 John 4:16b-21, vs. 16b: God is love, and he who abides
in love abides in God, and God in him.*

Object: an eraser, popcorn, a napkin.

Good morning, boys and girls. Today we have a
lesson that I know you are all going to enjoy. Of all the
questions that I hear people ask about God, this is the
easiest one to answer. It is also the most fun to tell
people about because they always like the answer. Now
the question is this: "What is God really like?"

Now, before I tell you the answer to the question, I
want to show you how I like to explain it. In my hand I
have a couple of things. I want you to tell me what they
are really like. First of all, I have this pencil with an
eraser on the end of it, and I want you to tell me what
this eraser is really like. [*If you have several children,
you could divide them into groups to answer the questions.*] Now, the answer is simple, so don't make it too
hard. What is an eraser really like? While you are thinking about the eraser, let me ask you about something
else. What is popcorn really like? That's the second
question, and here is a third one like it. What is a napkin
really like? Now, who can tell me the answers to these
questions? [*Let them all make guesses at an answer.
Give them some clues so they feel as though they have
participated in the search.*]

Well, here are the answers. An eraser is like rubber;
popcorn is like corn; a napkin is like [*Let them guess.*] —
that's right — paper. Rubber, corn, and paper.

Now, what do you think God is really like? [*Let them
guess.*] God isn't rubber and he isn't corn and I know that
he isn't paper, so what is he?

God is love. That's right, just like popcorn is corn and
napkins are paper and erasers are rubber, so God is love.
That is what God is really like because that is what God

is made of. Isn't that wonderful? The thing that we like best of all, love, is what God is made of and because he is love we are happy and safe and, if we believe in him, we can also be filled with love. I am glad that God is love and not corn or paper or rubber. I can't touch him, or squeeze him, or eat him, but I can love him and that is the best part of all. When someone is full of love, he is kind and generous and helpful. Well, God is all love and he is the kindest, most generous, and the biggest helper the world has ever known.

The next time someone asks you what God is really like, you can tell him that he is love, but first show him how you know just as I have told you today.

NOOSES OR BABY BOTTLES?

1 John 3:13-18, vs. 14: We know that we have passed out of death into life, because we love the brethren. He who does not love remains in death.

Object: a rope in the form of a noose, and a baby bottle.

Good morning, boys and girls. It is a wonderful thought to get up every morning and thank God for all the good things that he has given us and particularly for the wonderful life that we have to live. Of course, the Bible teaches us that living is more than just breathing. Living according to God is loving.

Let me show you what I mean. Here is something that I am sure all of you have seen in the movies or on TV. [*Hold up the noose.*] Who knows what you call a rope that is tied like this? [*Wait for the answers.*] It sure is a scary-looking piece of rope, isn't it? You know what people do with ropes like this, don't you? That's right, they hang other people who have done wrong things. Hangman's ropes are a sign of hate. They mean the end of life and no one wants to have his life ended that way, but when people lie, their lives become filled with hate, and they sometimes die this way. That is bad and we feel badly for people who hate because they miss all of the good things that God wanted us to have on his earth.

Now here is something else that all of us know about because we have often seen it. [*Show them the baby bottle.*] This is the sign of new life. When you see a baby bottle, you think of someone who is not only tiny, but also someone who is loved. A baby is not only new life, he is also a loved life. This is the way life should really be.

God says that people who love other people are showing the real meaning of life as Jesus taught it. When we love others, we are trying to help them live their lives the best way that a person can live.

When we share, we teach others to share. When we forgive, we teach others to forgive, and when we help others, we teach them to help. This is love and it is also life. That is the way God teaches us to use our lives. There is no room for hate and, as long as we have no hate, then we never have to worry about things like ropes, particularly ropes with a noose at the end. All we have to do is love others, as we love a baby, and our lives will be filled with joy and happiness.

DANDELIONS AND ROSES

1 Peter 5:6-11, vs. 6: Humble yourselves therefore under the mighty hand of God, that in due time he may exhalt you.

Object: a dandelion and a rose.

Good morning, boys and girls. How many of you know what it means to be humble? [*Listen to their definitions.*] A humble person is someone who doesn't think too much of himself and would rather give the credit to someone else.

I want to tell you a story about two flowers that I think you will enjoy and from which I hope you will understand the meaning of humility. This is the story of two flowers, Ruby Rose and Dorla Dandelion. Ruby Rose was hard to live with. She was always reminding everyone of her unbelievable beauty and the special kind of care that she needed. Ruby needed her branches trimmed regularly, some spray to keep away the bugs, and special kinds of food put into the flower bed in which she lived. Ruby was quite a flower and, on occasions when she thought that no one like you and me were listening, she would tell all of the flowers how wonderful it was to be a rose. Most of the flowers in the same yard with Ruby could not stand her, but Dorla never said anything unkind about her. When new flowers would come into the yard, Dorla would always introduce them to Ruby and tell them of what fine stock Ruby came from and how beautiful she was when she was in full bloom. Now, there was only one thing that Ruby wanted that she didn't have. It was upsetting that it took her so long to come into full bloom, and then several days later she would fade out and it would take a while for her to have another beautiful bloom.

Ruby was her nastiest when she would make remarks about Dorla getting old and gray. How Ruby would like to stand tall in the garden and look over the yard and tell Dorla how awful she looked with her fuzzy gray hair. But Dorla would never say anything unkind back. Instead, she would tell Ruby how wonderful it was to have such a beautiful flower like her in the same yard, even if she couldn't live with her in that wonderful flower bed.

Now, let's see how God works things out for us. The one thing that Ruby always despised about herself was how hard it was for her to have rose friends. It seemed like it took forever for her to have any new friends. She used to secretly wish that she could have one real rose friend and not have to talk to weeds like Dorla.

What Ruby didn't know was God's special plan for Dorla. You remember those old gray hairs that Ruby made fun of every day? Well, God made those gray hairs seeds so that when the wind came and blew away the gray it made fields of new Dorlas, so many that the proud Ruby could not even count them.

That is the way God works with the proud and the humble. It may not seem right to be humble all the time, but God rewards the humble with gifts so great that it is by far the very best way to be.

DO THE TOUGH THINGS FIRST
(For use on the Sunday nearest July 4)

Romans 8:18-23, vs. 18: I consider that the sufferings of this present time are not worth comparing with the glory that is to be revealed to us.

Object: a shovel and a bucket.

Good morning, boys and girls, and how are you on this very important day in the history of our country? How many of you know what day today is and what happened on this day? [*Let them tell you about the Fourth of July.*] That's wonderful that you know so much about this important day. Are there any other days like this that you can compare the Fourth of July with, so I will really know how important it is? Do you know what I mean by comparing? [*See how many know what the word means.*]

Let me show you what I think would be a good example of the word compare. Do you see this shovel and bucket? Well, let us suppose that we were going to build a swimming pool. How many of you would like to have a swimming pool that you could swim in every day? Oh, boy, all of you. Do you like to swim and lie in the sunshine? Well, before you can do that you are going to have to dig and dig and dig. Does that sound pretty good? You are going to have to dig all this summer, but next summer you will have a place to swim. You wouldn't mind digging all summer, would you? Of course, next summer you would have to carry buckets and buckets of water until the pool was filled up so that you could swim in the water. You wouldn't mind carrying a bucket of water, would you? [*If you can, have the bucket filled with water so they can feel how heavy it would be.*] Pretty heavy, isn't it? But just think, after the pool is filled, you can swim and swim. You see, I am comparing the work that it would take with the fun it would be to have a place to swim whenever you wanted to.

That's the way St. Paul looked at the problems that he had with being a Christian. Oh, he thought being a Christian was pretty tough sometimes, but when he thought that God was going to give him the most wonderful life he could imagine, he thought there was no comparison. Paul told everyone that he would take the tough problems of being a Christian now for a little while because he knew that God was going to let him enjoy life forever.

It isn't easy to forgive someone who has hurt you, but you can do it if you know that God wants you to and it will help everyone be a better person. You see you have to compare what might be a little suffering now with what will be a joy forever. It would be better to dig and carry water for one year if you got to swim in a pool for twenty years than not to dig or carry water at all. The same is true with being a Christian. You will do the tough things now and know that you are going to live with God forever.

PLAYING GOD'S GAME

1 Peter 3:8-15a, vs. 11: Let him turn away from evil and do right; let him seek peace and pursue it.

Object: games like dominoes, jacks, or pick-up sticks.

Good morning, boys and girls. Today we are going to have a good time because I brought with me some games that I know all of you like to play. How many of you have ever been allowed to play a game during church and not have someone look at you with a big frown on his face? [*Give them your very best look of scorn.*] Well, today, I brought along some of these games that I used to play and perhaps some of you still play today. Here is one of my favorites, called pick-up sticks. How many of you know how to play pick-up sticks? Very good. Here is another that I played a long time ago, but was never very good at. It's called jacks. You have to be very quick at this game if you are going to win. Is there anyone who has ever played jacks? Some have and you know how quick you must be. This last game is really an old game and people used to play it a lot, but you don't see it much anymore. The game is dominoes. Is there anyone here who has played this game? I don't think so.

Well, this certainly was a fun morning playing all of these games, wasn't it? [*The fact that you haven't played one will bring their objections, but just go on talking about how much fun it was to play and mention their names and talk about winners, etc.*] Yes, it has been a lot of fun, but that is what games are for, aren't they? I mean, they let us have a lot of fun. [*Now you hear them.*] What do you mean, we didn't play the games? We talked about them, didn't we? In other words you are telling me that if we want to play the game we have to do more than just talk about it.

I wonder if that is what God means when he tells us about peace. I hear people talking about peace all the time, but very few of the people who talk ever do anything about it. They don't pursue it as God says that we must. If we want peace, then we have to do something and not just talk about it. We have to forgive and share and love and help and work hard if we want peace. If we want to play pick-up sticks, we have to take them out of the box. Well, that certainly is something to remember. You have to do something to play the game and you have to do something if you want peace. Maybe you can remember this, too, and help bring peace to God's world.

FREE FROM SIN

Romans 6:3-11, vs. 7: For he who has died is free from sin.

Object: a slide and a slide projector.

Good morning, boys and girls. I want to talk to you this morning about something which we don't often like to talk about. The subject is death. Now, most people are afraid of death. They don't know what it is about, so they are afraid of it. It only comes to you once, and after it happens, there is nothing else that we know like it. I suppose if you only got a chance to eat once, you would be afraid of it also. Now, we know that God makes certain promises to us about what happens when we die, and we certainly hope that they are true. One of the things that God tells us about living is that, as long as we live, we have to live with sin. It is a part of life and while we don't like it, we still have to live with it. God also promises that after we die we will not have to live with sin any longer. I want to show you why I think that life will be better after we die than it is now.

I have in my hand a slide. I took this slide while I was on vacation and I think that it is beautiful. I am going to pass it around and let everyone take a good look at it. [*Pass it to each child and even hold it up to the light so that they can see there is something on the slide.*] This is the way that I think we are today, before we have died. You and I can look at this slide and we know that something is on it, but it is very dark and hard to see. The darkness, or the part that makes it hard to see is what we can call sin. Now, I am going to take this slide and bury it in my projector. Let's pretend that the slide with all of the sin has died. You remember how dark it was and how hard it was to see. Now, when I turn on the light it will be like God coming for us after we have died. God is going to take away all of our sin. [*Turn on the projector.*] Isn't that a beautiful sight? Do you see how clear it is and free from the darkness of sin? That is the way that I think that God is going to make it for you and me after we die. I think that we are going to be free forever from the darkness that makes it hard to see and believe today. So, you can see how wonderful it is going to be when God calls us to live with him and be free from sin forever.

TOUGHER THAN BUMPERS

1 Corinthians 4:9-15, vs. 10: We are fools for Christ's sake, but you are wise in Christ. We are weak, but you are strong. You are held in honor, but we in disrepute.

Object: a car bumper (borrowed from a junk yard).

Good morning, boys and girls. How many of you know what an apostle is? Can you tell me who was an apostle? [*Allow them some time to answer.*] An apostle is a special disciple, one of the very first believers who was chosen by Jesus to help him in his ministry. Some of the apostles had names like Peter, and John, and Andrew. One of the apostles was a man named James who had a brother named John. John was a fisherman. The apostles had a very difficult job, because they had to be some of the very first people to teach others about Jesus. It wasn't always a very pleasant task.

I brought with me this morning something that reminds me of the kind of people apostles had to be. How many of you know what this thing is? That's right, an automobile bumper. It fits on the front of the car and it has a very special job. How many of you know what a bumper does? That's right, it protects the car's fenders, and radiator, and lights, and a lot of other things. It always has to go first and people always know that when they see the bumper there is a car following it. A bumper has to be rugged and tough and take a lot of punishment, but it also has to tell others that it is leading something which is not far behind.

That was the job of an apostle. He had to be rugged, no sissy, and he had to be a leader, so that other people knew that what they were telling meant that the Christian faith was coming to their town or city or village.

The apostles did a good job and they were all tougher than any bumper ever made when it came to taking the abuse and punishment of people who did not want to hear and learn new things about God. St. James was one of those men and we are glad for what he did. Because he was willing to go ahead, teaching the good news, and was willing to suffer if he had to, we are able to be Christians today in a world that now knows a lot about Jesus and the love of God. That is why we have a St. James Sunday and I hope the next time and every time that you see a bumper from now on you will think of James and the other apostles.

THE DEVIL IS A MOSQUITO BITE

Romans 8:12-17, vs. 12: So, dear brothers, you have no obligations whatever to your old sinful nature to do what it begs you to do. (The Paraphrased Epistles)

Object: a mosquito bite.

Good morning, boys and girls. There are certain things that I like about the summer and there are a few that I am not so happy about. Tell me some of the things that you like best about the summer. [*Let them tell you about not having to go to school, being able to swim and play ball.*] That's very good. Is there anything that you don't like about summer? That's a pretty hard question, because we always think about summer as being a time of fun and we all like fun. Let me tell you something that I don't like and see if you don't agree with me. I don't like mosquito bites. Is there anyone here this morning who has a mosquito bite? [*Bring forward your volunteer.*] Why don't you like mosquito bites? Doesn't that feel good when you first get a mosquito bite and you scratch it? Oh, boy, I can just feel it now. I know that if I scratch that itch just a little bit, it will feel so good. But then what happens? That's right, you scratch it so much that it begins to hurt. The only way to make a mosquito bite go away is to leave it alone or it will soon become very sore.

Mosquito bites just beg you to scratch them, but you know that you must not do it. The same is true about our lives as St. Paul teaches us. There are certain things that always look like they would be a lot of fun, but our experience teaches us that we will only get into trouble if we try them. Our parents tell us to stay close by while all of our friends are going away. What shall we do, listen to our parents whom we know are right, or listen to that voice inside of us that is just begging for us to go? Sometimes we see something that we know does not belong to us, but we are sure that we would never be caught if we took it. Should we leave it alone or should we listen to that voice that begs us to take it and use it the way we want to use it? St. Paul teaches us that there are better ways to live after we become Christians and that we should always follow them, even when we hear the old ways begging us to do it like we did it before. The devil is like an old mosquito bite that keeps begging us to scratch, even when we know that pretty soon the itch will turn into a bad sore. So remember, don't scratch mosquito bites, and don't listen to voices that beg you to do what you know is wrong. That is what a Christian must remember at all times if he is to grow strong in the Lord.

God promises to strengthen us and help us if we ask Him too

GOD'S THERMOMETER

1 Corinthians 10:1-13, vs. 6: Now these things are warnings for us, not to desire evil as they did.

Object: a thermometer.

Good morning, boys and girls. Today I would like to talk with you about something which we all know a lot about. I want to talk to you about warnings. Can anyone tell me about something that we all know is a warning? Maybe some kind of signal or something like that. While you are thinking about your warnings, let me show you something I brought along that helps us know a warning. [*Hold up the thermometer.*] What do you call this? That's right, a thermometer. I suppose all of you have noticed that when you are not feeling well, your mom or dad comes over and touches your head. If you feel even a little bit warm, the next thing you know they are putting this thermometer in your mouth and waiting to see what your temperature is. Is there anyone here who knows what your temperature should be if you are all right? That's right, 98.6, and so if your temperature reads 100.4 or 101.2, or something like that, then your parent sees this as a warning and calls the doctor for an appointment or gets you some medicine in a hurry or both. The thermometer gives the warning.

God gave us and still gives us a lot of warnings, and sometimes we pay attention to him and sometimes we don't. People used to ask St. Paul why certain things happened to God's children. They wondered why the Jewish people were captured or why they had to spend forty years in the wilderness. St. Paul said that God allowed these things to happen so that we would be warned. We should learn from other people's mistakes and take them as warnings so that we don't do the same things. If someone shows you a scar and tells you that he cut himself by holding the knife wrong, then you will remember that and won't hold the knife that way. When God tells us that there are certain things that happen to people who don't obey his laws and don't treat people with love, he is warning us about how we should live.

Maybe you can think of some warnings now that we have all heard about. [*Let them tell you about a few warnings.*] That is very good, and maybe you will also now remember why God warns us. He doesn't want us to get hurt or to suffer. Instead, he wants us to be happy and healthy. So you do as the people did with St. Paul. Learn God's warnings and obey him and you will have a wonderful life.

SHARING GOD'S GIFTS

1 Corinthians 12:1-11, vs. 11: All these are inspired by one and the same Spirit who apportions to each one individually as he wills.

Object: a map of the United States.

Good morning, boys and girls, and how are you today? Have you ever wondered why some people can do some things better than you can and why you can do one or two things better than anyone else? You have? Did you know that God planned it that way and that the whole world is about the same way? I mean there are some boys and girls on the other side of the world who wonder why some children can do things better than they can. They also know that there are one or two things that they can do better than anyone else in the neighborhood.

I suppose you know that this doesn't happen only to people. Let me show you what I mean. Here is a map of the United States. How many states are there in the United States? That's right, fifty. Are all fifty states important? Could we just give away Florida or Minnesota and still have the United States? Of course not. Every state is important and every state contributes something important to the other forty-nine. For instance, if we didn't have Florida, then we would miss having a lot of oranges and grapefruits and lemons and other fruits. Or, if we gave away Minnesota, then we would lose a lot of the iron ore that the rest of the country needs. Ohio makes a lot of glass, and Michigan makes cars, and Washington makes wood for houses. Every state is important and we must always remember how important they are. Now, there is some oil in Ohio, but not as much as there is in Texas. They grow trees in Ohio, but not as many or as big as they do in Washington and Oregon.

That is the way it is with people. Some people can do a lot of things, but they do only one or two things very well. God gave everybody some talent, but no one has all of the talent. No one of our states has more of everything than any of the other forty-nine. God wanted everyone to be able to do something very well, so that other people would need him. But he gave no man everything so that every man would need other people. You know what you can do very well and God wants you to share your gift with others. He also wants you to use the things that other people have so that they know that you need them.

SALT SHAKERS AND YOU

1 Corinthians 15:1-10, vs. 10: But by the grace of God I am what I am, and his grace toward me was not in vain. On the contrary, I worked harder than any of them, though it was not I, but the grace of God which is with me!

Object: a salt shaker and some salt.

Good morning, boys and girls. Today we are going to find out how wonderful we really are, and at the same time how really wonderful we could be if we knew something that St. Paul discovered a long time ago. I have a friend who has a collection of salt shakers, and she has brought them home from all over the world. Many of them do not look like salt shakers, but that is what they are. I brought one of her very beautiful salt shakers with me this morning so that you could see what a pretty thing it is. How many of you would like to have a salt shaker like this on your kitchen table? It is a handsome one. There is only one problem with this salt shaker. I wonder if anyone here can tell me what it is? [*Let them examine the shaker and guess what might be wrong with it.*] Has anyone discovered the problem? That's right, it needs salt. What good is a salt shaker without salt? None at all. But suppose I open it up and pour some of this inside and then what do we have? A really beautiful salt shaker.

St. Paul discovered a long time ago that he was a very talented person. He was smart, he could write well, he understood languages, and he could do almost anything that he wanted to do. There was only one thing missing, and when he received that, he felt that he was for the first time a complete person. That thing that made Paul someone whom we remember is called grace, God's grace. It is kind of like the salt in the salt shaker. Without the salt, the shaker is pretty good to look at, but not really complete until we add the salt. We are all human beings, but what makes us special is that we are filled with the grace of God. When we are filled with that grace, we are able to do things that God wants us to do. If we do not have God's grace inside us, then we cannot do what God wants us to do.

We have to be open, ready for God to fill us up like we did with the salt in the salt shaker. When we have his grace, we are able to do all of the good things that we always dreamed of doing but never thought possible. So, get filled up, not with salt, because that is for salt shakers, but get filled up with GRACE!

CONFIDENCE IN JESUS·

*2 Corinthians 3:4-9, vs. 4: Such is the confidence that we
have through Christ toward God.*

Object: a bottle of perfume.

Good morning, boys and girls, and how are you
today? Isn't this a wonderful way to start out a new
week? I like to be together with you in God's house.
Today we are going to talk about a very special word —
confidence. How many of you have ever heard of the
word confidence? Some of you have. What do you think
the word confidence means? [*Wait for some of their
definitions.*] Those are pretty good. Let me show you one
way to explain the word confidence. Let's suppose that
your father called up on the phone and asked your
mother to go out with him tonight to a very special
restaurant and then see a very special movie. Do you
think that your mom would like to go? You think that she
would. Fine. Now, what do you think that your mother
would do? I think that she would get all cleaned up, put
on her prettiest dress, and then just for an extra special
touch she would add her confidence. Do you know what I
mean by her confidence? I think that she would put on
just a little bit of this. [*Show them the perfume bottle.*]
Would you like to take a little smell of her confidence?
Doesn't that smell good? No question about it, your dad
would know that your mom is really extra special and
she would feel very confident that he would be pleased
that he had asked her to go out. Perfume gives a girl
confidence.

Jesus Christ is confidence also. He doesn't smell like
perfume, but we know that when we have Jesus within
us we cannot fail. We know that God is going to love us,
care for us, and provide a home for us forever when we
have Jesus and his teachings in our hearts. Jesus is the
confidence that we need to do anything that we want to
that is good.

Now, we can't just put Jesus on and take him off like perfume, but it is Jesus and our belief in him that makes us special people to God. Jesus did everything right and God appreciated that. Jesus said that he would share himself with us in such a way that we could be confident that God would love us just like God loved him. So now you know what confidence means. We never have to worry about God's loving us again, because we have Jesus in our hearts.

The next time you see your mother put on some perfume, you will know that she is adding her confidence and then you will think about how good it is to have Jesus in your heart. How wonderful it is to know that God loves you just like he loved Jesus.

GOD REMOVES WRINKLES

2 Corinthians 3:4-9, vs. 5: Not that we are sufficient of ourselves to claim anything as coming from us; our sufficiency is from God.

Object: a coat hanger.

Good morning, boys and girls. It surely is good to come to church on Sunday mornings and share some of our time with our friends. How many of you have friends here at church? That's good. What is a friend like? [*Allow them to answer.*] Those are some good answers. Are friends good to have around sometimes when you need help and somebody to depend on? Sure they are. I brought a friend with me this morning whom all of you are going to like and maybe this friend is just like one of your friends at home. I call my friend Curly — Curly Coat Hanger. That's kind of a funny name, but that's what he likes to be called, so we all call him Curly at our house. How many of you have someone like Curly at your house? Everyone, that's good.

Now, Curly is a good friend all of the time, but he is especially good to my clothes. Sometimes I come home and take my coat off and just put it on a chair or lay it on the bed. That seems so easy and I always plan to hang it up, but somehow the minutes and hours pass and my coat still lies on the bed or the chair. When I pick up my coat and put it back on again it doesn't look so good. Do you know what is wrong with it? [*See if they can guess.*] That's right, it is wrinkled and it looks like a mess. Sometimes I blame my coat and complain about the way it was made or the material that was used to make it, but I really know that the wrinkles are my fault. A coat needs help if it is not going to wrinkle. That is where our friend Curly Coat Hanger comes in and does the job. The coat cannot hold itself up so that the wrinkles will hang out, but a coat hanger can make my coat look like it was brand new, or at least pressed.

God is like that with you and me. Sometimes we think that we don't need to do what we should do. And we get wrinkles, too; but we call these wrinkles sins. We can't get rid of them any more than our coat can get rid of the wrinkles by itself. So, we need something that makes us strong, and that something is God. God is like Curly the Coat Hanger. When we depend on God, we get rid of all our wrinkles, or sins, and we feel much better. God is strong and we can depend on him all day, every day. So, the next time you see your friend who is like Curly, you think about God and say to yourself, "I know that I can depend on God to get rid of all my sins and give me new strength."

MUSTARD ON MASHED POTATOES?

Galatians 5:16-24, vs. 17: For the desires of the flesh are against the Spirit, and the desires of the Spirit are against the flesh, for these are opposed to each other, to prevent you from doing what you would.

Object: salt, vinegar, and mustard.

Good morning, boys and girls. Have you ever tried to hit a ball with a tree branch or walk barefooted on a very hot sidewalk or hot sand? If you have, you know that some things just don't go together. You need shoes to walk across something that is hot and you need a bat to hit a ball. Those things are made to go together and the others are not. I brought along some other things that you know a lot about that I think will help you understand one of God's teachings this morning.

Here are three different things that you put on your food at different times. [*Hold up the three so that everyone can see them.*] What do you call this yellow stuff in this jar? That's right, mustard. And how about this white liquid in this bottle? Vinegar. Okay, now tell me what I have in this container with the holes on the top of it which is like white sand when I shake it out? Salt, very good. Have you ever tried to put salt on bread when you thought it was sugar, or mustard on mashed potatoes, or drink a glass of vinegar when you thought it was water? If you ever have done anything like this you know how terrible it is. Mustard and mashed potatoes, or salt and bread, just don't go together, and vinegar will never replace water.

St. Paul teaches us that the same thing is true about our wishes and what God wants for us as well. Very often our wishes are selfish. Sometimes we would like to just punch that guy in the nose, but God wishes that we would reach out and help him get another fresh start. Our ways and God's ways are different many times. St.

Paul teaches us that whenever we know what God would
do and what he wants us to do, that we should do it God's
way and save ourselves a lot of trouble.

God's way teaches us to put salt on meat and vege-
tables, instead of on bread; and God teaches us to put
gravy, instead of mustard, on our potatoes, so you can
see that God's way is right. Seriously, I know that you
sometimes feel that it would be better to punch the
fellow in the nose, but really, it would be better if you
loved the guy even more now that he has done something
to you. So, you remember that the things that go well
together are the things from God and you will then
remember to do the right thing in Christ's name.

YOU CAN TRUST GOD

Galatians 5:25-6:10, vs. 25: If we live by the Spirit, let us also walk by the Spirit.

Object: a walking stick or cane.

Good morning, boys and girls. Today we are going to let one of our friends help us learn something about God. This is not a brand new friend. I imagine you have seen him many times before. As many times as you have seen him, though, you have probably never used him. His name is Kerry Cane. Good old Kerry has been a lot of help to a lot of people. Why, I can remember when Kerry helped my next door neighbor learn to walk again after he broke his leg. My neighbor used to lean on Kerry real hard, but Kerry never let him down. I can remember another time when a friend of mine who was blind lost his own cane and he used Kerry to feel for furniture and walls in my house, when he walked around. Kerry was a lot of help and you can depend on Kerry to do the job.

Being ready to help is not limited to my friend Kerry Cane. No, sir. The Spirit of God can be depended on also. The Spirit will always do for us what is right. Sometimes God tell us that we need to depend on the Spirit when things get rough and we do not think that we can do it all alone. We like to brag that we can do the job or overcome the pain or problem without anyone's help. But God says that that kind of bragging, or being conceited, is foolish. We should depend on God's Spirit to help us just like my friend, who had the broken leg, leaned and depended on Kerry. There are other times when we can't see what is going to happen if we try something that God is asking of us and so we are afraid to do it. God says to us that we should give at least ten cents of every dollar to his special work in our offerings. But a lot of times people think that they cannot afford to give that much back to God and still pay their bills. God says trust me like a blind friend trusted Kerry to point out the furniture and walls and everything will work out. If we can walk in trust, then we can live in trust.

So, the next time that you see Kerry or someone like Kerry, you remember the kind of trust people have to lean on and follow a cane and then you think to yourself, "If that man can trust a cane and not be afraid, then I can surely trust God and not be afraid."

GOD ANSWERS THE TOUGH QUESTIONS

Ephesians 3:13-21, vs. 19: And to know the love of Christ which surpasses knowledge, that you may be filled with all the fulness of God.

Object: a slide rule, a cookbook, and a map.

Good morning, boys and girls. Isn't it wonderful that we know so much about so many different things? It is also amazing that the things we don't know about somebody else does. Where do we get all of our answers? Let's suppose that you wanted to have a chicken dinner today, but you wanted it fixed differently than you have ever eaten it before. What will your mother do? I know what she will do. She will go to her cookbook and look up all of the ways there are to fix chicken and then let you choose your way. Let's suppose that you have a very difficult arithmetic problem to figure out and you just can't find the answer with any of your methods. What will you do? You may take your problem to an engineer and he will take out his slide rule and in a very short time will give you the solution. Here is one more way that you can find an answer to a most difficult problem. Suppose that you wanted to go far, far away and you didn't know how to get there. What would you do? I know what you could do. You could get a map and find out where the city is where you wanted to go. Then you could pick out the road you wanted to travel on. That is the way that you figure out those kinds of problems.

But suppose you wanted to forgive someone for hurting you, or suppose you wanted to live after you died? Now, who do you go to? Where do you get answers like that? When you or your mother are sick and you need special attention, who do you call?

Sometimes we have to depend on someone who knows more about things in this life than the smartest man or all of the books in the world. Do you know who I am talking about? That's right, God. The love of Jesus is greater and goes further than anything that we know in the whole world. When the problem is really tough and there are no answers in books or people, we have to turn to God to get the answer. When you know how much God loves you, then you can forgive anybody for anything that they might have done. When you know how much God loves you through Jesus, then you quit worrying about dying because you know that Jesus can give life forever, even after you die. And when you are sick or you feel all alone at night, you are never afraid because Jesus promises you that he will come and be with you and share every moment with you as long as you need him.

Sometimes we are pretty smart, but when it comes to the real tough questions, then we need the love of Jesus for the real great answers.

DRIED PAINT AND HARD BREAD

Ephesians 4:17-28, vs. 26: Be angry but do not sin; do not let the sun go down on your anger.

Object: a can of dried paint and a piece of dried bread.

Good morning, boys and girls. Today we are going to talk about something that all of us know about, because we have all been like this at one time or another. Have you ever been angry? Sure you have, because everyone gets angry about something. You don't have to fall on the floor and stamp your feet or throw things around the room to show that you are angry. You can be angry inside and never show it, or you can shout and scream and knock things over, and still be angry. St. Paul teaches that it is all right to be angry with people when they are wrong, but he cautions us never to sin in our anger. If you are angry because things are not the way you want them to be and you hurt someone, then you have sinned in your anger. But St. Paul says that you may be very angry when you have been hurt or had trouble in one of many ways. Just don't sin!

There is one thing that Paul teaches us about anger, though, that is very important, and I want to teach that to you today. Look what I have here in my hand. [*Show them the paint can and the dry piece of bread.*] Do you know what is the same about both the paint and the bread? Take a good look. You may even feel them if you would like so that you will know how paint and bread can be alike. Now, do you know? [*See if any of the children can make the connection.*] How would you like to try to paint your house with this paint? You couldn't? Why not? Because it is dry and you couldn't put it on a brush. That's very good. How about the bread? Who wants to take a bite of this bread? You can't because it is too hard. How do the paint and bread get so hard that you can't use them? By leaving the lid off the paint and the bread out of the bread sack. That's right.

St. Paul teaches us that we should never go to bed at night angry. By the time the sun goes down, we must get over our anger. Do you know why? For the same reason that you can't leave the lid off the paint and the bread out of its wrapper. Your anger will get hard and you will get hard with it. Your anger will hurt you, if you let it stay in you overnight. Anger is to be used to get rid of the awful feelings that are inside of you and then it is over with and put away. Never stay angry overnight or you will turn into something that you will not like. The man who left his paint can lid off overnight or the woman who left out this piece of bread were sorry, but there wasn't anything that they could do about it. Use your anger, but never let the night pass without getting over it. Okay? Okay!

MAKING THE MOST OF TIME

Ephesians 5:15-21, vs. 16: Making the most of the time because the days are evil.

Object: an appointment book.

Good morning, boys and girls. Today we are going to talk about something that is very important to us all. It isn't money, or ice cream, or hamburgers. It isn't riding a bike or playing dolls. We aren't going to talk about school or taking a bath. But, you couldn't do any of these things if you didn't have the thing that we are going to talk about this morning. We are going to talk about time. How many of you know what time is? [*Let them answer.*] Those are some pretty good answers. Time is very important and it can help us a lot if we know how to use it.

I brought with me today a very good friend named Aaron, Aaron Appointment Book. Now Aaron keeps me pretty busy most days. The first thing that I do when I get up in the morning is to take a look at Aaron to find out how I am going to use the time God has given me. At 9:00 I must meet with Mr. Brown, and at 10:00 I promised that I would be at a very important meeting where lots of money is going to be spent. At 11:00 Mrs. Jones is going to be operated on at the hospital and I promised her that I would be there in time to have prayer and wait with her husband and talk to the doctor. This afternoon I must teach a class at the church and meet with the organist. The time goes fast when we use it the right way. Time is important and so is Aaron. If I didn't have Aaron, I might go to the church in the morning to teach my class and miss the meeting and Mrs. Jones. Aaron helps me stay on schedule and use my time right.

God teaches us that we are going to do something with the time that we have and that, if we don't plan it wisely, we will soon find ourselves wasting it. Pretty soon we will use the time that God has given us to do wrong things. That is why it is so important that we use and plan our time well. Every Sunday you can plan on coming to church for a couple of hours and that is a good use of your time. You don't have to wait until Sunday to use some of your time to pray and do kind things for your friends and help your mother. You can do these things anytime. There are all sorts of ways that boys and girls can plan their time and make good use of it so that you are pleasing to God. By the way, you should plan some play time, because God thinks that every boy and girl should have some play time. But learn to use your time wisely and you will be as glad and happy about life as Aaron is when he is all filled up without even one empty line.

LET JESUS FORGIVE YOU!

*Romans 3:21-28, vs. 25b: This was to show God's right-
eousness, because in his divine forebearance he had
passed over former sins.*

*Object: a magnifying glass, a piece of wood, and some
wood filler.*

Good morning, boys and girls. Is anybody perfect?
We would all like to think that we are pretty good, but
we know that none of us is perfect. As a matter of fact,
there is practically nothing perfect about us. We are a lot
like this beautiful piece of wood that I have in my hand.
When you look at it from where you are sitting, it looks
pretty nice, almost perfect. The wood is smooth and the
grain is lovely. But suppose you took this ordinary
magnifying glass and gave the wood a close look. What
do you think you would find? Why don't you look with
me? [*Bring the children in close and show them the imper-
fections.*] Do you see the little holes in the wood and the
changes in the grain? You do? That's good. That piece of
wood is a lot like us. No matter how good we look from a
distance, we all have the same problems when you look
closely.

God calls these problems sins. If God wanted to play
the game by the rules, we would be in big trouble. Every
time we did something wrong God would have to
remember it and punish us for it. In other words, God
would have to keep score and make us pay. But the Bible
teaches us that God is not like that. We don't pay for our
sins because God gave us Jesus, and Jesus died for all of
our sins. When Jesus died, he covered over all of our
holes and blemishes and made us smooth. Jesus is kind of
like this wood filler that I have in my hand. You see,
when I take this paste and rub it into the piece of wood,
all of the holes are filled. When the paste dries and
becomes hard, there will be no holes and you will not be
able to find any, even with a magnifying glass.

That's the way Jesus is for you and me. We have our sins and there is nothing that we can do to get rid of them. But Jesus can get rid of them, and he does this by forgiving them and making us perfect in the sight of God. That's why we are so happy to have Jesus. He makes us perfect when we can't do it ourselves.

The next time you see some holes in a piece of wood, you can remember that the holes in wood are like sins. The only way to get rid of the holes is with wood filler and the only way that we can get rid of our sins is to let Jesus forgive them.

GOD'S MARK ON YOU

Revelations 7:2-17, vs. 3: Saying, "Do not harm the earth or the seas or the trees, till we have sealed the servants of our God upon their foreheads.

Object: six cans each of four different kinds of soft drinks.

Good morning, boys and girls. I hope that none of you is mixed up this morning. Is everyone at the place he wanted to be when he left home this morning? There isn't anyone here who thought he was going to a ball game or a movie or another church, is there? Good, everyone is where he should be.

It is important that we are where we belong, isn't it? Let me show you what I mean. [*Bring out the different kinds of soft drinks with all of them mixed up in different cartons.*] Now, one look at this and you can tell we are in a mess. Is there anyone here who can help me out and get my soda pop straightened out? [*Choose a volunteer.*] How can you tell where they each belong? [*Let him answer.*] By their labels or marks! Very good. Let's see, one of them says Pepsi Cola, one is Seven Up, one is Coca Cola, and one is Root Beer. Coke goes with Coke, Pepsi with Pepsi, etc. Now I see. And you can tell where they belong by their labels. It is no accident when they are all in the same carton.

Did you know that it was not an accident that you became a Christian? God called you. He put his mark on you. There isn't a sign on you that reads Christian, member of St. Luke's Church, but God has marked you in his own way. That's right, he knows who you are and that you belong to him. The day you were baptized you became a Christian and God marked you as one of his own. To God you are better marked than a Pepsi, Coca Cola, Seven Up, or Root Beer.

It was no accident that you became a Christian. Someone brought you to God because he loved you and cared about you, and when God received you, he marked you forever. You can't see the mark, but God can and he will never forget you. Never. You belong to him for good.

ADDRESSES AND CHRISTIANS

Philippians 3:17-21, vs. 17: Brethren, join in imitating me, and mark those who so live as you have an example.

Object: an envelope addressed correctly and an envelope addressed incorrectly.

Good morning, boys and girls, and how are you today? Are you all fine and happy to be here this morning? Good, I knew you were. Did you know that every Sunday morning when you get up and come to Sunday School and worship, you set a good example? Of course, when you sleep in or stay home and read the funny papers you set a bad example. St. Paul wrote a lot about setting a good example.

Let me show you what I mean. Here are two envelopes with letters in them. One of the envelopes is a good example and one is a bad example. [*Hold up the envelopes.*] Which envelope is the good example? That's right, this one is the good envelope. The bad envelope has the stamp in the wrong corner, the street address is on one side and the name and the city are upside down. If you used this envelope as an example, your letter would never get to the place you wanted it to go. That is the way it is with people. Your friends will never come to our church if you set a bad example and stay home to read the funny papers. People will not see Jesus in you if you only talk about forgiveness, but never forgive those who hurt you or your feelings.

Now, if you address your envelopes like the good example, your letters will always arrive where you want them to go. That is the same way that people become Christians. People want to be Christians when they see and know good examples of Christianity. This envelope is addressed correctly. The Christian example is a boy or girl who loves people, worships God, is always ready to forgive and help other boys and girls.

We want you to be good examples of the teachings of Jesus. Just as good envelopes reach the right address and person, so Christians who do what Jesus teaches arrive in God's kingdom.

GOD'S TIME IS DIFFERENT

2 Peter 3:8-14, vs. 8: But do not ignore this one fact, beloved, that with the Lord one day is as a thousand years, and a thousand years as one day.

Object: a scale, some sheets of paper, and a brick or stone.

Good morning, boys and girls. Have you ever wondered if God listens to your prayers or cares if you do something good for someone else? You would be very unusual if you did not wonder about it. We all know that God answers us and cares about us, but we wonder sometimes if it doesn't take too long. The Bible teaches us that we should never be impatient with God, for he always does everything at the right time for us and for him. Time is important to God, but it must be a little different for God since he lives forever. The Bible says that one day is like a thousand years and a thousand years to us is just like one day to God. That's really different. One day is very important to us and none of us will ever live to be one thousand years old. But the Bible says that they are the same to God.

Let me show you what I think this means. Do you see the one-pound mark on the scale? When something weighs one pound, it shows up here on the scale. If I take this rock and put it on the scale it weighs one pound. Just one rock weighs one pound. But, if I want paper to weigh one pound, I have to put this many pieces on the scale. [*Put several pieces on at a time until you reach the number.*] It takes one hundred pieces of paper to make one pound, while it only took one rock. A rock is like a hundred pieces of paper and a hundred pieces of paper is like one rock.

God will always answer your prayer. If it needs to be answered in one day, God will answer your prayer in one day. If it needs a thousand years, then God will take a thousand years to answer your prayer.

94

God is the same to you and me as the pound is to paper and stone. We will never worry about God changing or not caring about us. God will always care and do for us what needs to be done no matter how long it takes or how small it may seem. God will always be with us.

HOW MANY CIRCLES 'TIL JESUS COMES?

Romans 13:11-14, vs. 11: Besides this, you know what hour it is, how it is full time now for you to wake from sleep. For salvation is nearer to us now than when we first believed.

Object: a tree log.

Good morning, boys and girls. Have you ever thought of the many ways there are to tell time? There are watches and clocks, as well as sundials, to tell the hour of the day. We have calendars to tell us the day and the year. Today I have brought with me a very special kind of time teller. [*Hold up the log.*] Did you know that you can tell time with a log? Sure you can. Who knows how to tell time with a log? [*See if one of the children can tell you.*] That's right, there is a circle for every year that the log lived as a tree. Our log lived for five years. Do you see how the circles get closer together as they get nearer the center of the log? The closer that you get to the time when the tree was born the smaller the circle. Five circles, all coming closer and closer to the moment of birth.

You know that someday Jesus is going to return to earth as God promised. With every day that comes and goes, we get closer to the time that Jesus will return, just like the circles in the log. Now the Bible teaches us that we must believe that Jesus is Lord and that God is waiting for just the right time to send Jesus back into the world. Until Jesus comes, we are told that we must carry on as Jesus taught us. That means that we are to love others, forgive them when they do wrong to us, and help everyone who needs our help.

No one knows how many new circles there will be on the trees until Jesus comes again. Only God knows if there will be one, five, ten, a hundred, or a thousand new circles. The only thing that we do know is that we are closer to the time now than we were yesterday. We pray that Jesus will come to us soon, but we will believe and act as he taught us until that time comes.

BE STEADFAST IN GOD

Romans 15:4-13, vs. 4: For whatever was written in former days was written for our instruction, that by steadfastness and by the encouragement of the scriptures we might have hope.

Object: the heartbeat of each child.

Good morning, children. This is the first Sunday of the most exciting month. How many of you know what month this is? That's right, December. It seems that all of the other months, like January and July and October, are in the calendar so that they will get us to December. I know that you like December because of a very special day. What day do you like so much that comes in the month of December? That's right, Christmas.

There is something else that gets us to December every year that is even more important than the dates or months on a calendar. I want you all to choose a partner and be very quiet so that you can listen for a steady sound. [*Let them all select some partner.*] Now, I want you to take turns and listen for a sound that you can hear in each other's chest. [*Show them by letting someone listen to your chest and vice versa.*] Do you hear that beat? What is that sound that you hear? The heart, that's right, and your heart sounds exactly like your partner's heart. Did you notice how steady it is? Thump, thump, thump, over and over again your heart beats out the same rhythm. We could call your heart "steadfast." Can you say that word with me? "Steadfast."

We must be steadfast, too. Day after day, year after year, the Bible tells the same story of the wonderful things that God did and still continues to do. When we are sad, joyful, afraid, excited, or however we feel, we should read the Bible and listen to God's teaching. Even now while we are waiting for Jesus to come and be born in our world again, the place that we go to look for him is the Bible. The Bible gives us hope. So remember this: The Bible teaches us to be as steady and dependable as our heart is. God wants us to be in rhythm with him. The next time you listen to a heart beat, remember how good it is for us to be steadfast in God.

GOD'S X-RAY VISION

1 Corinthians 4:1-5, vs. 5: Therefore do not pronounce judgment before the time, before the Lord comes, who will bring to light the things now hidden in darkness and will disclose the purposes of the heart. Then every man will receive his commendation from God.

Object: an X-ray. (This may be borrowed from almost any doctor or hospital.)

Good morning, boys and girls. Things are certainly happening fast, aren't they? The time seems to fly faster and faster while we wait for the big day that is coming. How many of you are ready for Christmas? That's good.

Today we want to talk a little bit about judging. St. Paul said that it isn't good for us to judge one another. Do you know what I mean? We should not say that a person is good or bad. Perhaps what St. Paul really meant was that we should not try to make up our minds whether or not someone is a good Christian or a bad Christian. St. Paul says that the judging belongs to God. The reason that we should not judge is that we don't know all of the facts about why people are the way they are.

Let me show you what I mean. Sometimes things are hidden from us and we don't know why people do the things that they do. For instance, if you went to a doctor with a bad pain in your side, or your foot hurt really badly, what do you think the doctor would do? Do you think that he would just say, "Let's operate for a hole in your tummy or let's wrap your foot in a bandage?" Of course not, even if he had a good idea of what was bothering you, he would say, "I think we should take an X-ray of your side or your foot." The doctor wants to make sure.

Now, let's look at an X-ray. If you just look at the X-ray as I hold it next to me, you will not see a thing. But if I hold the X-ray up to a bright light, then look at what you can see. With an even brighter light like they have at the hospital or a doctor's office, you can see even better. I can't see your bones from the outside, but if I had an X-ray of you I could tell you what your bones looked like.

That is the way it is with God and his judgment. God is the bright light and when we are held up to him, he can see and make a true judgment. We don't have that bright light, so we cannot be judges of other people. Other people's lives are like an X-ray without a light to us, but they are like an X-ray held up to a bright light for God.

GOD'S SUGGESTION BOX

Philippians 4:4-7, vs. 6: Have no anxiety about anything, but in everything by prayer and supplication with thanksgiving let your requests be known to God.

Object: a suggestion box.

Who has a suggestion box? My suggestion is that we sing more songs on Sunday morning and that my friends sing louder and with great joy. That's my suggestion, what's yours? [*See if the children have any suggestions of any kind.*] Do you all know what a suggestion is? [*See if you get any answers.*] A suggestion is an idea of how to make or do something better. Some churches, schools, factories, and other places have a suggestion box and the people who work there are asked to contribute their suggestions. The people put their suggestion in the box and someone answers the suggestion.

Maybe you don't want to suggest that something be done differently, but you may just need an answer to a problem or a situation. Another word we must learn is the word request. Suppose you wanted the day off from school and you ask your mother to write a note and request that the teacher excuse you the next day. A request is something that we ask of someone else. You can make your requests known in the suggestion box, too. You can request that the teacher show more movies, or give you more time for gym. Now, it is up to the teacher to answer your request with either a "yes" or a "no."

The Bible teaches us that we can make requests of God. Instead of worrying and fretting over some problem, the Bible teaches us to request the answer from God.

Let's look in our request box or suggestion box and see what kind of requests there are. [*Reach into the box and pull out some slips with some requests written out.*]

102

Here is one that says, "God help me quit smoking." Is
there anyone at your house who wants to quit smoking
and may have asked God for help? Here's another one,
"Dear God, give me the courage to stop watching
television when I should be studying." How about this
one, "Please Jesus, give me the strength to do the dishes
without fighting with my brother and making my mother
angry."

These are just some of the requests and you probably
have your own. Maybe, when you go home today, you
would like to put up your suggestion box so that you
could write out your requests to God. It will help you and
God will love hearing from you often.

GOD'S RIGHT PLAN

Galatians 4:1-7, vs. 4: But when the time had fully come, God sent forth his Son, born of woman, born under the law.

Object: a doll with a pull string that makes her talk.

Merry Christmas to all of my Christian friends. The Christ Child is born and we are all filled with joy over his coming. I want you to know that the birth of Jesus was no surprise to God, nor was it any accident that he was born here on earth. Jesus came as the result of a plan that God made and kept. Jesus came because God wanted him to be our Savior.

How many of you know what I mean when I tell you that God kept his promise? What does it mean to keep a promise? [*Wait for the replies.*] That means that God did what he told us that he would do. He said that one day, when it was just the right time, he would send his Son into the world. The time was God's time.

Let me show you what I mean. How many little girls got a doll for Christmas? Did anyone receive a doll like this? [*Hold up the doll so that they can see; they probably will be able to tell you the name of the doll.*] There is something very special about this doll, because she can do something that a lot of dolls cannot do. Who can tell me what this doll can do that is special? That's right, she can talk. Do you know how this doll talks? That's right, by pulling a string. But you have to pull the string all the way out or it will not work. Watch! [*Pull the string part of the way several times.*] You must pull the string all the way. That is the way the doll talks and a lot of other things work. You must go all the way.

God waited for just the right time. He didn't send Jesus into the world at this time [*Pull the string out a little bit and then a little further each time as you talk.*] or this time, or this time, but only when the time was

full, just right. That's why I told you that Jesus came as
the result of a plan by God. The Bible says that God sent
Jesus when the time was full, just like when I pull the
string all of the way out. Not until it was complete and
the plan was perfect did God give Jesus to the world.

The next time you think that God sent Jesus a long
time ago and you wished that he would send him now
instead of then, you remember what you learned today.
When the string was pulled all of the way, the doll could
speak, and when the plan was just right God gave Jesus
to our world.